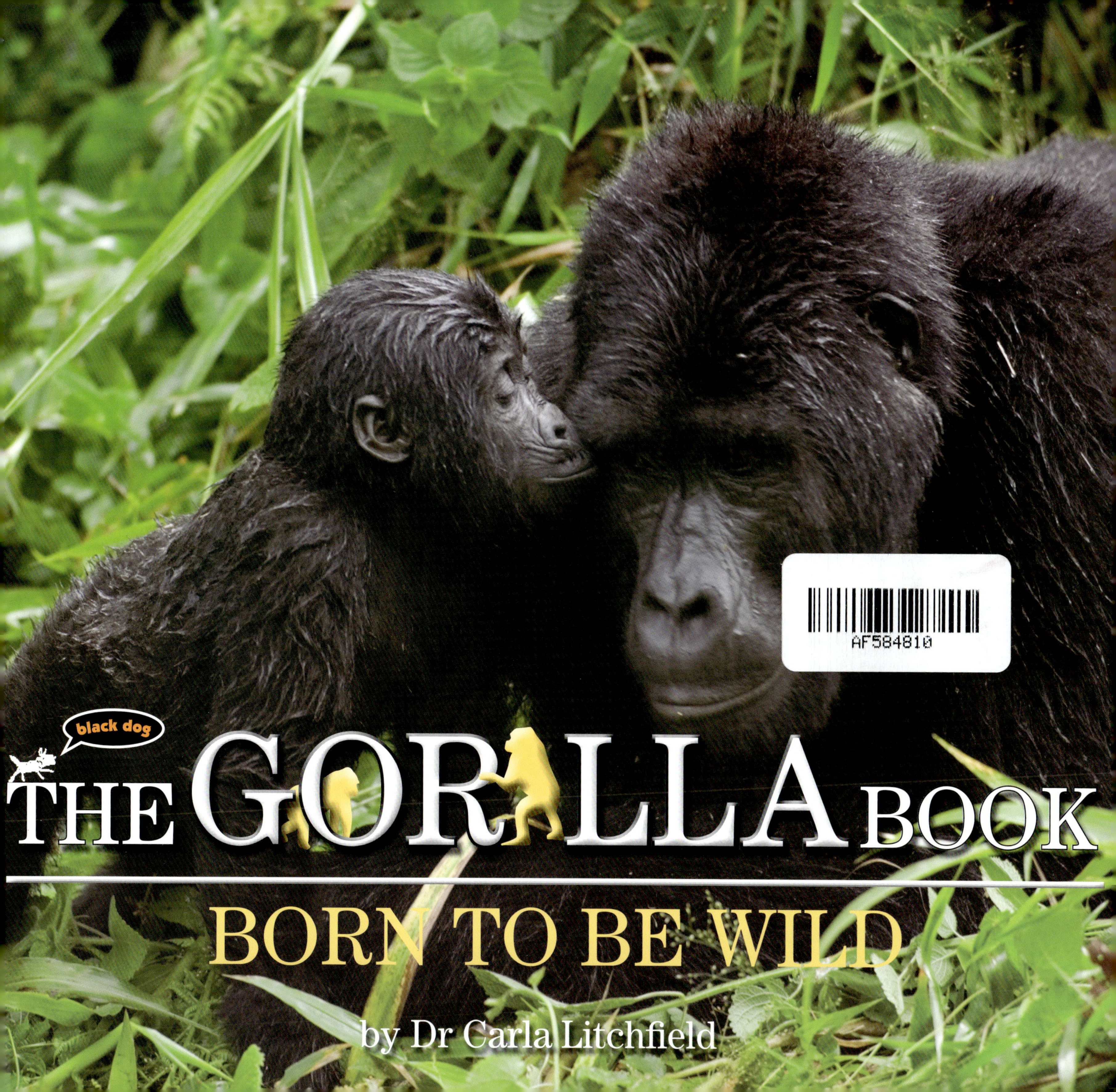

THE GORILLA BOOK

BORN TO BE WILD

by Dr Carla Litchfield

Dr Carla Litchfield is a scientist at ZoosSA, and lecturer at the University of South Australia. She has studied great apes in the wild and in zoos and sanctuaries around the world. She is the current President of the Australasian Primate Society.

To my wonderful daughter, Kaitie Afrika Litchfield. Thanks to the Nyakagezi gorillas at Mgahinga Gorilla National Park, Uganda, the first wild gorillas I spent time with. Also, to Safiri and Anguka, two wonderful gorillas who spent some time at Adelaide Zoo.

Photo credits:
DLLIL/Corbis: front cover, p i; shutterstock: pp i, ii, 2, 3, 7, 26, back cover; istockphoto: pp 4, 6, 9, 16, 18, 29; Suzi Eszterhas/Minden Pictures: p 8, Photolibrary: pp 9, 10, 11, 13, 21, 23, 27, 28; Adam K. Thompson/Zoo Atlanta: pp 11, 12; Dr Carla Litchfield: p 12, Yann Arthurs-Bertrand/Corbis: p 14; Dian Fossey Gorilla Fund: p 15; African Conservation Foundation: pp 20, 21; aapimages: pp 24, 25, 27, 30

p 19: 'Leah', Breuer T, Ndoundou-Hockemba M, Fishlock V (2005) 'First Observation of Tool Use in Wild Gorillas'. PLoS Biol 3(11): e380 Oct 2005

pp 17, 22, 29: Lucy Spelman for www.gorilladoctors.com

First published in 2009 by
black dog books
15 Gertrude Street
Fitzroy Vic 3065
Australia
61 + 3 + 9419 9406
61 + 3 + 9419 1214 (fax)
dog@bdb.com.au
Dr Carla Litchfield asserts the moral right to be identified as the author of this Work.

Designed by Blue Boat Design
Printed and bound in China by Everbest Printing

FSC is a non-profit international organisation established to promote the responsible management of the world's forests.

National Library of Australia
cataloguing-in-publication data:
Litchfield, Carla.
The gorilla book: born to be wild.

Includes index
For primary school children.
Subjects: Gorillas--Africa--Juvenile literature
Animal Behaviour--Juvenile literature
ISBN: 9781742030883 (pbk)
Series: Wild Planet
Dewey number: 599.884096

10 9 8 7 6 5 4 3 2 1 9/0 1 2

black dog books would like to thank Professor Colin Groves for his thorough factual check of this book.

KEY
On some pages you will find a sidebar which shows: how far above sea level gorillas live; the names of some other **primates** in the same area, and gorilla **predators**. This information is always changing due to war, disease, loss of **habitat** and poaching.

Part of the proceeds from this book will go to Conservation Ark, which supports gorilla conservation and Year of the Gorilla projects.

CONTENTS

OUR GENTLE RELATIVES

Gorillas are our largest ape relatives. They are great apes, like humans, chimpanzees, bonobos and orangutans. There are two **species** of gorilla, the Western Gorillas (*Gorilla gorilla*) and Eastern Gorillas (*Gorilla beringei*).

Gorillas are easily upset. They are the most emotionally sensitive and usually the most peaceful of all the great apes.

An adventure book with stories about fearsome monster silverbacks was published in 1861 by explorer Paul du Chaillu, who toured around Europe showing stuffed gorillas he had hunted.

Scientists outside Africa first learned about gorillas in 1847, from a Western Lowland Gorilla skeleton that doctor and missionary, Thomas Savage, brought to New York from West Africa. Museums around the world competed for dead specimens to put on display. These magnificent 'monsters' were so fragile, they rarely survived for long once captured for display in early zoos.

Today, thousands of people from all over the world flock to see gorillas in the wild. In just one year, a **habituated** group of Mountain Gorillas can have more visitors than any of us might have in our house in a whole lifetime!

The Greek word 'gorillai', meaning 'tribe of hairy women', appeared in an explorer's tale centuries ago, but Mountain Gorillas were only discovered by modern explorers about 100 years ago.

WHERE IN THE WORLD?

The giant Congo river separates Western Gorillas from their Eastern Gorilla cousins. They live more than 750 km apart.

Western Gorillas include the Cross River Gorillas and Western Lowland Gorillas. The Eastern Gorillas include Mountain Gorillas and Grauer's Gorillas. Cross River Gorillas live in a small area in Nigeria and Cameroon. There are less than 300 of these gorillas.

Perhaps 200 000 Western Lowland Gorillas live across seven African countries. About 380 Mountain Gorillas live in the Virunga volcanoes area (Uganda, Rwanda and Democratic Republic of Congo) and about 320 at Bwindi Forest (mainly in Uganda). Fewer than 10 000 Grauer's Gorillas are found in Democratic Republic of Congo.

Virunga volcanoes, Rwanda

It is hard to estimate gorilla numbers. Many live in human war zones, or die suddenly in large numbers due to disease epidemics. The **Ebola** virus is a massive threat to Western Lowland Gorillas.

Gorilla gorilla diehli
Cross River Gorilla

Gorilla gorilla gorilla
Western Lowland Gorilla

Gorilla beringei graueri
Grauer's Gorilla

Gorilla beringei beringei
Mountain Gorilla

GORILLA BITS

Males are called 'blackbacks', as they have only black hair until about twelve years old. Then they become 'silverbacks', with silver hair from shoulders to bottom. They also lose the hair on their chests.

Adult males have a dome on the top of their heads called a **sagittal crest.**

Adult males are much larger than adult females. This is called **sexual dimorphism**.

Males can weigh up to 181 kg in the wild, and up to 220 kg in captivity.

Both male and female gorillas walk on their knuckles.

Gorilla hair can range from dark brown in Western Gorillas to black in Eastern Gorillas. Western Gorillas have reddish-brown hair on their heads and necks.

Male and female gorillas have **opposable** thumbs and big toes.

Every gorilla has a unique 'nose print', with different shaped nostrils and wrinkles above the nose. This helps scientists identify individuals.

Males can be as tall as a human, standing up to 1.7 m when they are upright.

Males have long hair on their arms to make them look big and tough.

Females can be up to 1.5 m tall when they stand upright.

Females can weigh up to 98 kg—about half the weight of silverback males.

GORILLA ENVIRONMENTS: FOREST, SWAMP OR 'SALAD BOWL'?

A Mountain Gorilla baby

Mountain Gorillas are the largest of the gorilla species. They live in high **altitude** rainforests. Their hair is thick and long to protect them from the cold and their lungs are big so they can breathe in the thin air.

Mountain Gorillas live in a lush 'salad bowl' environment. They munch herbs, leaves and roots, love young bamboo shoots, and occasionally eat fruit. These gorillas usually travel only 500 metres a day, because everything they need is right where they live.

A Western Lowland silverback

West of the Mountain Gorillas are Grauer's Gorillas. They eat leaves, roots, stems and ants. These gorillas eat lots of fruit, which is sometimes hard to find. When fruit is scarce, they may need to travel more than two kilometres a day searching for food.

At lower altitudes, in rainforests with massive fruit trees, live the Western Lowland Gorillas. They eat lots of fruit, and love termites and ants. Fruit trees are spread over large areas, so Western Gorillas have the biggest ranges of all the gorillas, travelling about one kilometre a day. One group of gorillas might be in the trees feeding on fruit, while another group might be wading in a swamp feeding on herbs. Almost all the gorillas in zoos are Western Lowland Gorillas.

Cross River Gorillas live further north-west than other gorillas, in hilly **terrain** and fragments of tropical forest. They experience hot dry seasons where fruit is not available. They eat more tree bark and lianas (vines) than other Western Gorillas.

A Mountain Gorilla eating thistles

GORILLA PERSONALITIES

Each gorilla is different in looks, movement and personality. There are also differences in behaviour between gorilla groups.

Gorillas make different sounds to communicate with each other. The most common sound is the soft grunting used to stay in contact with everyone in the group. Babies cry and whimper if they want their mum's attention. If gorillas are annoyed, they 'cough'. If they are enjoying a meal, they show it with contented 'belch grumbles'. Some Mountain Gorillas even hum which sounds like singing! Gorillas chuckle and laugh when play-wrestling or if they are being tickled. Silverbacks give alarm 'barks' if they sense danger, and scream, bark or roar if they fight.

When a silverback stands up, hoots, smacks his chest and charges, maybe bashing at some plants as he passes by, he can look very scary. But this threat display is just to show how tough he is. It is usually a bluff, and no one gets hurt.

KEEPING THE FAMILY TOGETHER

Most gorillas live in family groups, with several females and their offspring. A silverback leads and protects the group.

Gorilla groups vary in size. One group of Mountain Gorillas was reported to have about 60 individuals!

Many Mountain Gorilla groups have more than one silverback. Western Gorilla groups usually have only one silverback. Other silverbacks may live alone, or in 'bachelor' groups if they don't have a group of their own. This can happen if a group splits up because the **alpha male** has died, or if a male grows up and leaves to create his own family.

Female gorillas leave their family and join another group when they are eight to ten years old. They can usually have a baby by the age of ten. Most females only give birth every four to five years, as babies need years to learn what food to eat, how to behave like a gorilla and how to survive in the wild.

GORILLA CULTURE

This photo shows a silverback named Rigo using a stick to get a treat from an artificial termite mound.

For decades, scientists studying wild gorillas didn't observe them using tools like their chimpanzee cousins. It was thought that maybe gorillas didn't need a 'tool kit' to find or process food. Yet gorillas in captivity often use sticks and other tools to get food or treats.

In a study of gorillas in zoos, Dr Tara Stoinski and her co-workers found different tool-using behaviours. Sukari, a female gorilla at Atlanta Zoo, uses sticks to get food out of her reach. An infant gorilla named Itebero, at a sanctuary in Democratic Republic of Congo, can smash palm nuts open with rocks. Maybe scientists just weren't in the right place at the right time to see gorillas use tools in the wild?

Sukari using a stick to reach a feeder which contains apple sauce.

Every evening, most gorillas build a nest to sleep in. Mountain Gorillas often build their nests on the ground, creating a comfy bed by bending plants in towards a centre. Females and young Western Gorillas often build nests in the branches of trees. At the Mondika site in Central African Republic and Republic of Congo, silverbacks sleep on the bare ground when the weather is hot, and females and young gorillas build nests in trees. Sometimes gorillas will build a nest for a lunchtime siesta.

Some gorillas even visit sunken caves. In 2006, rangers found members of the Kibirizi group of Mountain Gorillas in a hidden cave. The gorillas had to use vines, roots and vegetation to pull themselves out of the 10 metre deep cave! No one knows whether they use the caves as shelter, or to hide from **poachers**.

A Mountain Gorilla snoozing in a nest.

THE FAMOUS GORILLAS IN THE MIST

KARISOKE GORILLAS

Gorilla beringei beringei

Where:	Rwanda
Map Coordinates:	1°30'S, 29° E
Rainfall:	1800mm per year

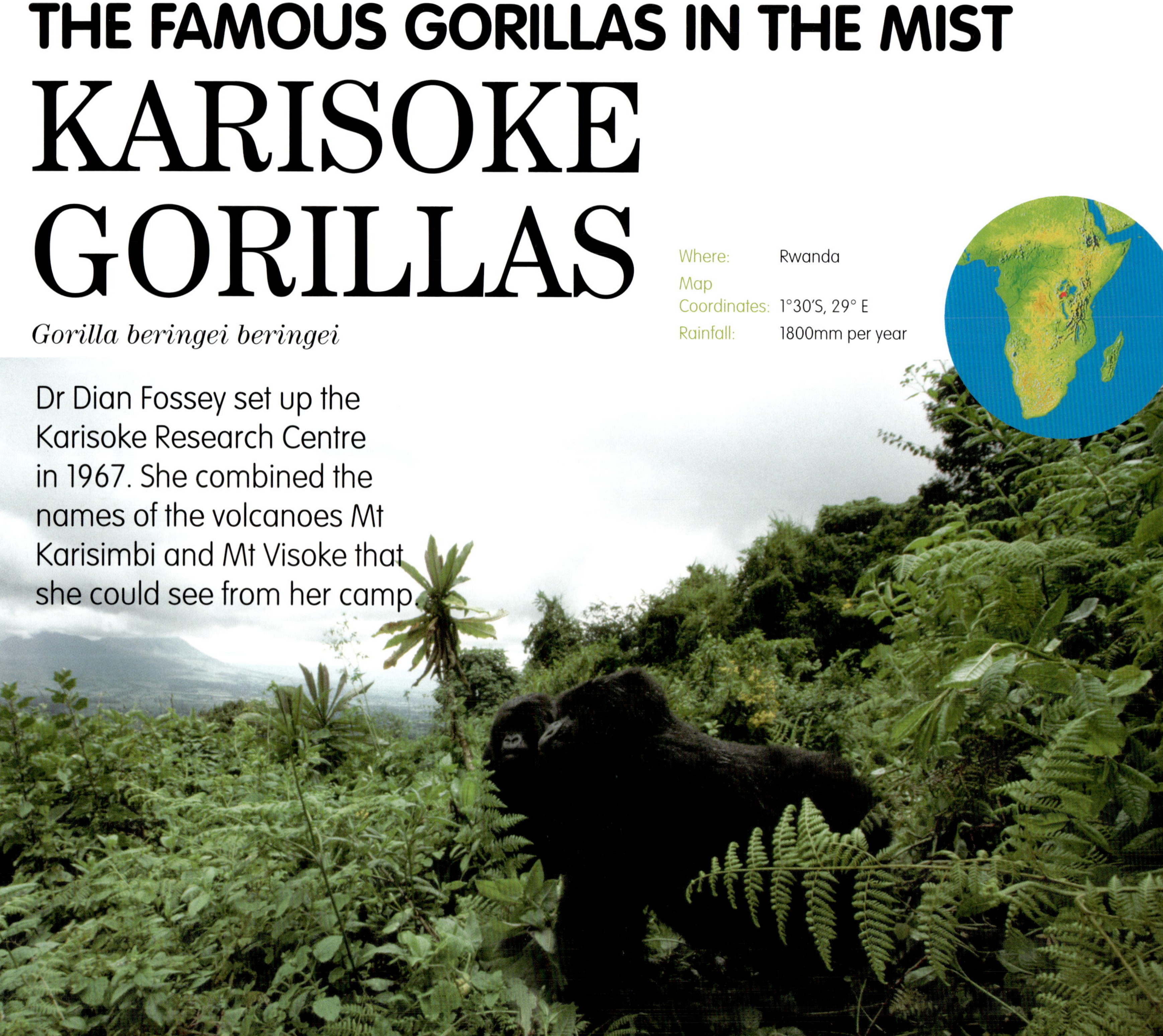

Dr Dian Fossey set up the Karisoke Research Centre in 1967. She combined the names of the volcanoes Mt Karisimbi and Mt Visoke that she could see from her camp.

Dian Fossey and Puck

Perhaps the most famous gorilla ever was Digit, a silverback at Karisoke. Dr Fossey had studied Digit since he was a youngster, a little ball of black fluff. Digit was killed in 1977, and Dr Fossey devoted the rest of her life to protecting gorillas. In 1985 Dian Fossey was killed, probably by poachers. She is buried next to Digit, her favourite gorilla.

Life in the wild for gorillas and scientists can be exciting—every day is a new adventure. The gorillas get to know the humans, and the humans know every gorilla by name, their personalities and life stories.

Dian Fossey started a long-term study of Mountain Gorillas after a visit to Africa in 1963. At first the gorillas were shy and frightened, but also curious about the tall woman following them. She helped the gorillas accept her by knuckle-walking near them like they did, and eating celery when they ate. For years she studied the gorillas, but could not ignore the poachers that came into the gorillas' territory. She wore scary masks to keep poachers away and burned their traps, methods that made her very unpopular.

Scientists at Karisoke still monitor three groups of mountain gorillas—Beetsme's group, Pablo's group and Shinda's group, all named after the silverbacks who lead them. Pablo was born in 1974. He was a mischievous youngster who sometimes stole notebooks or equipment from scientists. He later became a fearless silverback with his own group. Pablo even travelled ahead of his group to check dangerous areas for snares or traps.

4000m

Habitat:	Mountain rainforest and woodland
Predators:	Humans, possibly leopards

3000m

2000m

Other primate neighbours:	Golden monkeys, red-tailed monkeys, olive baboons and pottos
First studied by:	Dr Dian Fossey

1000m

Height above sea level

TROUBLE IN PARADISE
KAHUZI-BIEGA GORILLAS

Gorilla beringei graueri

In 1973, tourists began visiting habituated Grauer's Gorillas at Kahuzi-Biega National Park in the Democratic Republic of Congo. This rainforest paradise was listed as a World Heritage Site because it was considered so precious.

The silverback 'Maheshe' was the most famous gorilla in the country. His image with members of his family was even on the 50 000 Zaire bank note. Local people called their money 'Maheshe', and would say 'give me one Maheshe' when they wanted a note. When Maheshe was killed by poachers, the whole country mourned.

Where:	Democratic Republic of Congo
Map Coordinates:	2°S, 28°E
Rainfall:	1500-1900mm per year

In the late 1990s, war broke out. The Kahuzi-Biega National Park was added to the list of World Heritage Sites in danger. Today, uncontrolled mining for **Coltan** has pushed the remaining gorillas closer to extinction.

The home of Grauer's Gorillas contains up to 15 per cent of the world's deposits of Coltan. This space-age metal has allowed electronic devices, computers and mobile phones to get smaller. In 2001, as many as 10 000 miners moved into the area, hunting animals for food and degrading forests and streams. The **bushmeat** trade flourished, as did the illegal trade selling orphaned apes and other animals as pets.

Replacing your mobile phone every year, and constantly upgrading electronic devices, increases the demand for Coltan. Recycling mobile phones and electronic equipment can help save the gorillas.

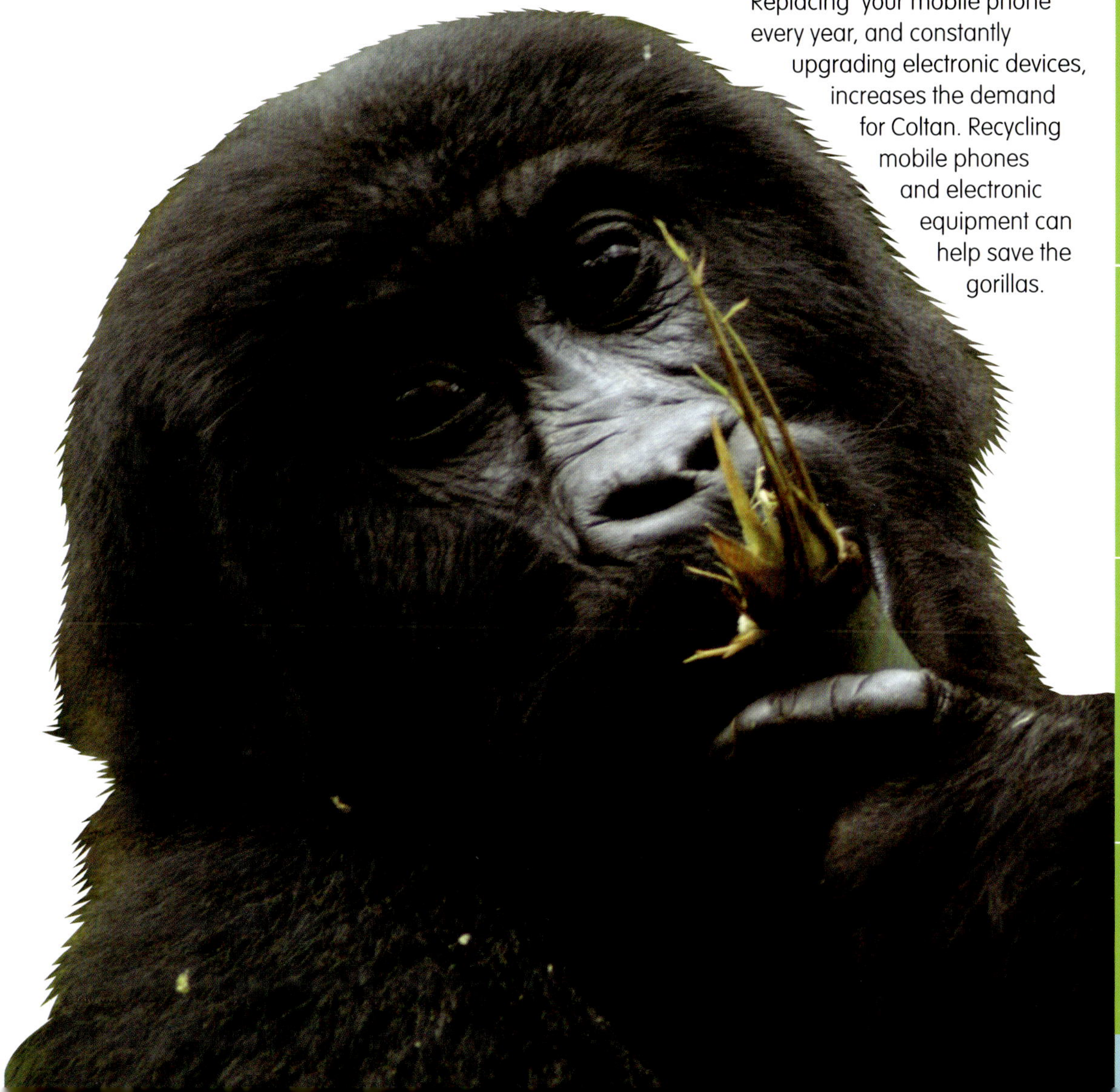

4000m

Habitat:	Subalpine rainforest, swamp forest, bamboo
Predators:	Humans, possibly leopards
Other primate neighbours:	Chimpanzees, red colobus monkeys, white-cheeked mangabey monkeys, red-tailed monkeys, Wolf's mona monkeys, olive baboons
First studied by:	Dr Juichi Yamagiwa, Dr Takakazu Yumoto, Dr Tamaki Maruhashi, Dr Ndunda Mwanza

3000m

2000m

1000m

Height above sea level

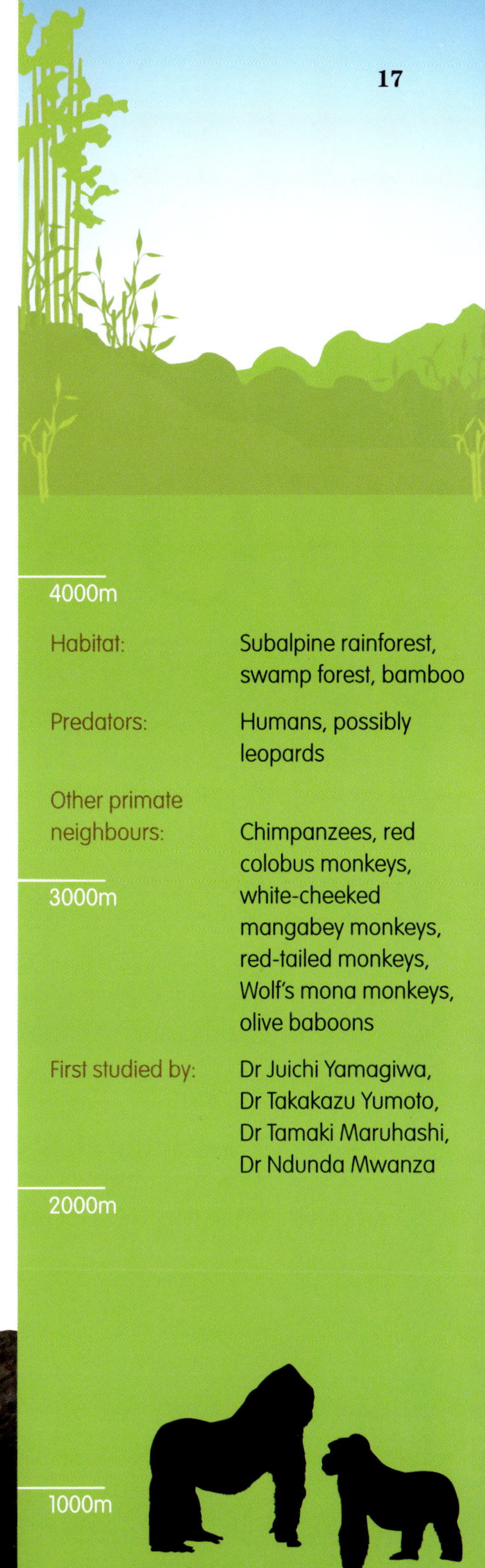

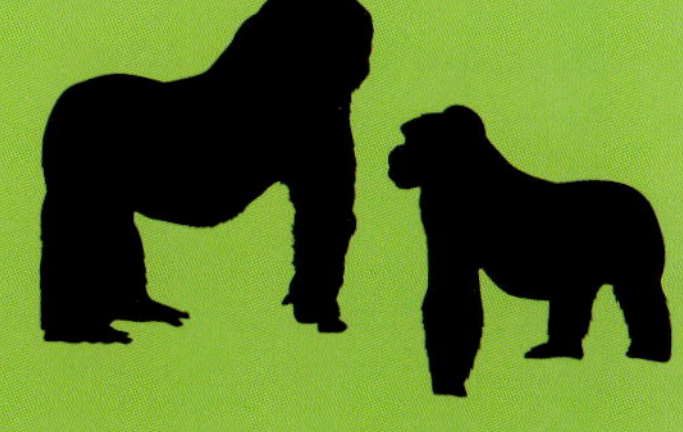

CROSSING WATER SAFELY

MBELI BAI GORILLAS

Gorilla gorilla gorilla

Most scientists study wild gorillas by following them on the ground. At the swampy Mbeli Bai site in Nouabalé-Ndoki National Park in the Republic of Congo, scientists have been observing gorillas through telescopes from a high platform.

At Mbeli Bai, scientists wait for hours every day for gorillas to come to the forest clearings, called *bais*.

Scientists have to be very patient, because on some days no gorillas turn up. On other days, two big groups can show up at the same time. It can take new observers months to learn to identify all the gorillas. Dr Thomas Breuer noted that in one year, 130 different gorillas visited the clearing. They belonged to 14 different groups, with another 13 solitary silverbacks. Elephants also visit the bais, as do shy forest antelopes like bongos and sitatungas.

Where: Republic of Congo

Map Coordinates: 2°15'N, 16°24'E

Rainfall: 1250mm per year

In 2005, scientists saw two gorillas use sticks to help them cross deep water and swampy ground. These were the first observations of tool-use among wild gorillas. While foraging for food, 'Leah' walked into the water until it was up to her waist. Then she broke off a branch and jabbed it in the water. She seemed to be testing the depth of the water, or how solid the ground underneath it was. Then using the branch like a walking stick, she safely crossed the water, collecting her crying baby waiting on the land.

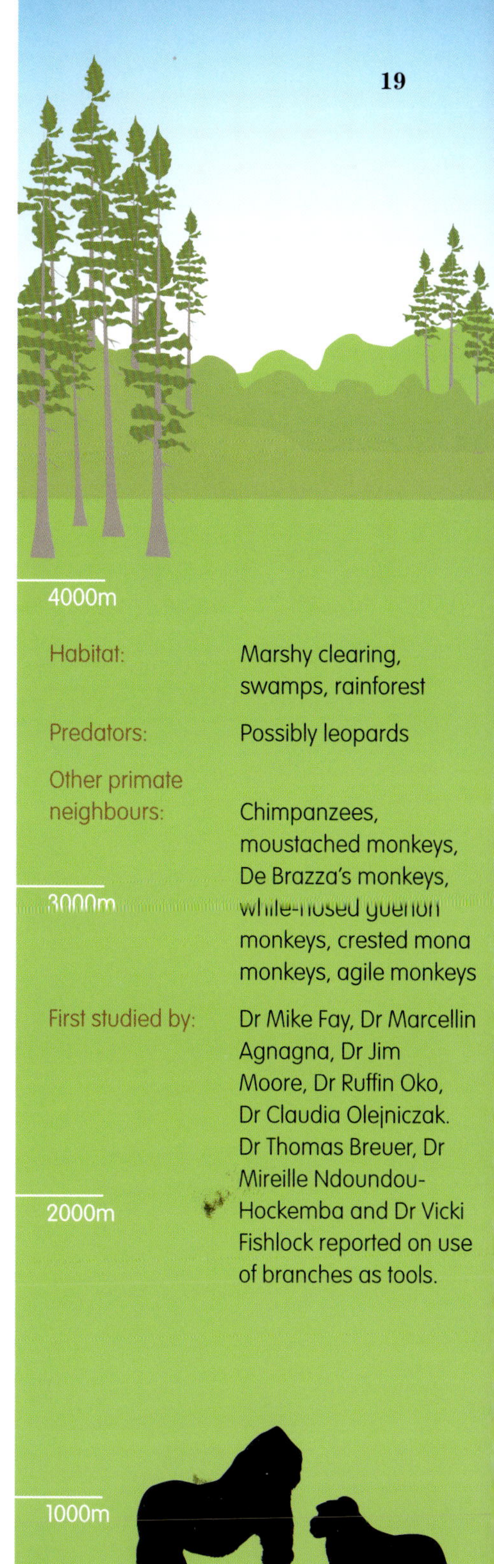

RAREST GIANTS

CROSS RIVER GORILLAS

Gorilla gorilla diehli

Where:	Cameroon & Nigeria
Map Coordinates:	9°45′ East 6°7′ North (Kagwene, Cameroon) & 9° East 6°20′ North (Afi Mountains, Nigeria)
Rainfall:	1500mm-3537mm per year

At the Kagwene site in Cameroon, Cross River Gorillas live near farms and human settlements. Scientists reported that some gorillas use an underarm technique to throw objects at people. The gorillas may have learned this from people throwing things at them to get them off their farms. Twice, while the silverback bluff charged, other gorillas threw clumps of grass and a large branch at scientists. Another time a man from a local village tried to frighten the gorillas off a path by banging his machete on the ground and throwing stones at them. Some of the gorillas tore up clumps of grass and threw them back at the man. The man then cut grass and threw it at the gorillas. This went on for more than an hour until the gorillas gave up and quietly left!

Cross River Gorillas are one of the 25 most endangered primate species in the world. Fewer than 300 of these gorillas live in areas scattered over the hilly regions near the Cross River, bordering Nigeria and Cameroon.

Cross River Gorillas are hard to study, because it is difficult for scientists to trek through their steep homes. These gorillas have also learned to avoid humans.

Habitat:	Lowland forest, sub-mountain & mountain forest, grassland, farmland
Predators:	Humans
Other primate neighbours:	Chimpanzees, drills, Preuss's monkeys
First studied by:	Dr John Oates, Dr Kelley McFarland, Dr Esteban Sarmiento, Dr L Wittiger and Dr Jacqueline Sunderland-Groves reported on object throwing.

4000m

3000m

2000m

1000m

Height above sea level

KWITA IZINA: NAMING GORILLA BABIES

Actress Natalie Portman named this gorilla 'Gukina', meaning 'play' in the local language.

Since 2005 in Rwanda, an annual ceremony has been held called **Kwita Izina**, to name baby Mountain Gorillas born in the Volcanoes National Park. Based on a Rwandan tradition of naming newborn babies, the first ceremony named one-year-old twins from the Susa group of gorillas. The President and the First Lady of Rwanda chose the name 'Byishimo', meaning 'joy' for the female, and her brother was named 'Impano' meaning 'gift'. These ceremonies recognise the importance of gorillas, and raise money for **conservation** and for people living in the area.

In 2007, 23 mountain gorilla babies were named by celebrities and visitors from all over the world. The celebrations included music, dancing and speeches—just like a giant birthday party!

THE SCIENCE OF GORILLA POO

Scientists can learn a lot from gorilla poo. Poo contains remains of food that a gorilla has eaten, and can have evidence of diseases. It even has the **DNA** of the gorilla.

From remains found in poo, scientists know that different gorilla groups eat different insects, and might use different techniques to collect them.

Scientists who follow wild gorillas always take along plenty of plastic bags. If they see a gorilla do a poo, they scoop it into a 'poo' bag, note down the gorilla's name, and pop it into their backpack.

More than 300 samples of poo were collected from Cross River Gorilla nests in Nigeria and Cameroon. DNA analysis of these samples showed that there were three main populations of Cross River Gorillas. Scientists were amazed, because the analysis showed that these three groups were related, and proved that some gorillas had travelled great distances, across roads, farms and grassland, to move to a new group. Scientists and conservationists can now try to plant more forest corridors to allow gorillas to travel safely.

Poo also provides DNA that can be used for paternity testing or finding out who is the father of a baby gorilla. The silverback leader is usually the father of the youngsters, but this is not always the case.

SMART GORILLAS: PROBLEM-SOLVING, THINKING AND COMMUNICATING

Everyday is a challenge for gorillas living in the wild. They have to find food, look out for danger and find a safe place to build a nest. Life in a zoo is almost the exact opposite—it can be too easy for these very smart beings! Everything is provided for them, and vets are on hand if they get sick or injured. This predictable environment can lead to bored, inactive or overweight gorillas. So zoos provide challenges to stimulate gorilla brains and encourage them to use natural behaviours.

Gorillas need to search for food hidden around their enclosure. Zoo keepers put treats in puzzle boxes or in empty plastic bottles so that the gorillas need some effort and skill to get them out.

Sometimes gorillas need to use a tool to push, pull or poke a piece of fruit out of a puzzle box. They can usually solve problems on their own. If they have trouble, they are shown the skill by a human so they can learn by imitation.

Scientists who study gorilla problem-solving in captivity use equipment that is bigger than that used by chimps or humans, because gorilla fingers are large and a bit less flexible than smaller apes.

A female Western Lowland Gorilla called 'Koko' has been using sign language to communicate with humans for more than 35 years. She makes up her own words, like 'finger bracelet' instead of 'ring'. When she signs the word 'love', it looks like a hug. She shows human emotions—she can be happy, jealous and sad. Koko is perhaps best known for her love of kittens, showing just how gentle gorillas can be. She named her first kitten 'All Ball'.

WHEN A SNEEZE CAN KILL

In the wild, tourists and researchers usually have to stay at least nine metres away from gorillas. Tourists come from all over the world, and might bring with them new germs. A common cold can be life threatening for gorillas, who might not have any natural resistance to it.

Gorillas are **genetically** close to us, so we can catch each other's diseases. By not getting too close, we are protecting both them and us.

To make sure that tourists don't disturb gorillas too much, visitors at Bwindi Impenetrable National Park in Uganda are only allowed to spend one hour with wild gorillas, and only eight people a day can visit each group of habituated gorillas.

When the park guides or rangers find gorillas, they make a special noise to let the gorillas know that friendly people are there.

Another problem with getting too close to gorillas is that they will lose their fear of humans. This can put the gorillas at risk of getting killed by poachers, because they will let the poachers get close to them as well. Gorillas might also start to visit farms to raid crops. Gorillas are much stronger than humans, so if they feel threatened, or decide to look at a tourist's backpack, a person might accidentally get hurt. Keeping a buffer distance protects people as well as gorillas.

KEEPING GORILLAS OUT OF TROUBLE

Gorillas sometimes live right next to fields where farmers grow crops like bananas and sweet potatoes. Once gorillas develop a taste for these foods they can get into trouble with farmers. When gorillas raid crops, they risk being caught in a trap, catching human diseases or even being killed. Farmers can lose their only source of income or food, and children sometimes can't go to school because they have to help protect crops.

Human-wildlife conflict is a real problem all around the world as wildlife habitats are destroyed so that humans can grow crops.

A Mountain Gorilla and rangers, Rwanda

The border between the Bwindi Forest and farmland. Gorillas can sometimes step straight out of the forest and into crops.

Volunteers living in villages around Bwindi Impenetrable National Park in Uganda have followed gorillas that leave the park. These Gorilla Monitoring and Response Teams are like neighbourhood watch groups, keeping gorillas and humans safe by chasing gorillas away from farms. They shout and whistle at the gorillas, and ring bells and herd them away from the crops.

Another way to keep gorillas away from tasty crops is to create buffer zones to separate national parks from farms. In these buffer zones, people can grow crops that gorillas don't like, such as chilli, wheat or medicinal plants.

GLOSSARY AND INDEX

Further Resources

The Dian Fossey Gorilla Fund International:

www.gorillafund.org/gorilla_fun/gorilla_sounds.php

www.gorillafund.org/gorilla_fun/for_kids.php

Year of the Gorilla 2009 and web links to projects supporting conservation activities:

www.yog2009.org

To find out more about national parks where wild gorillas live, and up-to-date information about conservation in the online *Gorilla Journal*:

www.berggorilla.de

For more gorilla sounds including humming/singing:

www.berggorilla.org/english/faq/dvers/hoeren.html

To find out how to help orphaned gorillas and other primates in Africa:

www.pasaprimates.org

For information on the Mountain Gorilla Veterinary Project:

www.gorilladoctors.com

www.mgvp.org

Glossary

alpha-male: the leader of a group.

altitude: height above sea level.

bushmeat: the meat of wild animals used for food.

Coltan: an abbreviation for columbite-tantalite, a metallic ore used in many electronic products.

conservation: the careful use and preservation of natural resources to prevent their destruction.

DNA: deoxyribonucleic acid, which contains the information about each living thing—what it is and what it looks like.

Ebola: a fatal disease in humans and other primates, characterised by high fever and bleeding.

genetics: the study of the variation of genes, which are passed from parents to children and may influence how we look and behave.

habitat: the natural environment of an animal.

habituate: to remove fear of humans. If gorillas keep seeing people who don't hurt or disturb them, they will gradually get used to having people around.

Kwita Izina: Rwandan ceremony held annually to name new baby Mountain Gorillas.

opposable: the tip of an opposable big toe or thumb can touch the tips of other toes or fingers, allowing the ape to grip things and pick them up.

poacher: a person who catches animals illegally.

predator: an animal that hunts or feeds on another animal (which is the 'prey').

primate: a group of mammals which includes great apes, humans and monkeys.

sagittal crest: the dome on the top of an adult male gorilla's head.

species: a biological classification for a group of organisms that interbreed and produce fertile babies.

sexual dimorphism: the variation in size between males and females of a species.

terrain: a piece of land or a geographical region.

vocabulary: a set of words that are understood or used as 'language'.

Index

Some things you can do to help save wild gorillas:

Buy plantation or recycled timber rather than tropical hardwood.

Recycle old mobile phones and electronic equipment.

Buy fair trade African products, such as coffee, tea or chocolate.

Support PASA sanctuaries, and help raise money for orphaned gorillas.